Jefferson Twp Public Library
1031 Weldon Road
Oak Ridge, N.J. 07438
phone: 973-208-6245
www.jeffersonlibrary.net

BRIGHT
IDEA
BOOKS

HOW DO ENGINEERS REUSE Rockets?

by Arnold Ringstad

Content Consultant
Daniel Kirk
Professor and Associate Dean for Research
College of Engineering and Computing
Florida Institute of Technology

CAPSTONE PRESS
a capstone imprint

Bright Idea Books are published by Capstone Press
1710 Roe Crest Drive, North Mankato, Minnesota 56003
www.mycapstone.com

Library of Congress Cataloging-in-Publication Data
Names: Ringstad, Arnold, author.
Title: How do engineers reuse rockets? / by Arnold Ringstad.
Description: North Mankato, Minnesota : Capstone Press, [2019] | Series:
 How'd they do that? | "Bright Idea Books are published by Capstone Press."
 | Audience: Grades 4 to 6. | Includes bibliographical references and index.
Identifiers: LCCN 2018018714 (print) | LCCN 2018024342 (ebook) | ISBN
 9781543541755 (ebook) | ISBN 9781543541359 (hardcover : alk. paper)
Subjects: LCSH: Rockets (Aeronautics)--Juvenile literature. | Aerospace engineering--Juvenile
 literature. | Astronautics--Juvenile literature. | Outer space--Exploration--Juvenile literature.
Classification: LCC TL782.5 (ebook) | LCC TL782.5 .R5275 2019 (print) | DDC 629.47/5--dc23
LC record available at https://lccn.loc.gov/2018018714

Editorial Credits
Editor: Megan Gunderson
Designer: Becky Daum
Production Specialist: Colleen McLaren

Photo Credits
AP Images: Refugio Ruiz, 23; NASA: 14–15, 28, Bill Ingalls, 13, Blue Origin, 24–25; Newscom: Cover
Images, 26–27; Shutterstock: Mykola Mazuryk, cover (background); SpaceX: cover (foreground),
4–5, 6–7, 8–9, 11, 17, 18–19, 20–21, 30–31

Design Elements: iStockphoto, Red Line Editorial, and Shutterstock Images

TABLE OF CONTENTS

CHAPTER 1

A THRILLING
Landing

It is a calm day at sea. The sky is blue. The waves are gentle. A wide, flat ship floats and bobs. A huge white X is painted on it.

High above the ship, a 120-foot
(38-m) rocket falls to Earth. Wind whips
around it. The rocket drops like a
stone. Suddenly, a bright flame shoots
downward. A loud cracking sound rips
through the air. Metal legs fold out.

The rocket is ready to go back to land. It can be used again later.

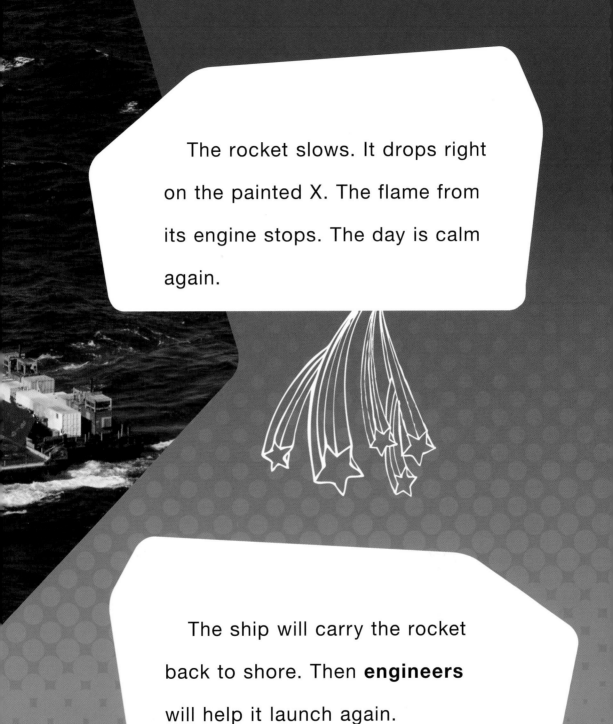

The rocket slows. It drops right on the painted X. The flame from its engine stops. The day is calm again.

The ship will carry the rocket back to shore. Then **engineers** will help it launch again.

CHAPTER 2

ROCKETS AT Work

Rockets are vehicles. They travel into space. Some carry **satellites**. Others carry people. All rockets use **propellant**. The engines burn it. Hot gases shoot out of the engines. This moves the rocket forward.

Rockets carry supplies to astronauts in space.

The first rocket went to space in 1957. It launched from the **Soviet Union**. Since then there have been many launches.

Many rockets are used once. They run out of propellant. Then they fall to Earth. They crash into the ocean. New rockets must be built. This takes time and money. Reusable rockets are cheaper. Engineers inspect each rocket after it lands. This makes space travel safer.

In the past,
rockets were
used just once.

Atlantis was the last space shuttle used.

Reusable rockets are not a new invention. Space shuttles are one example. They flew from 1981 to 2011. The shuttles had wings. They could land like airplanes. But they needed many repairs after each trip. They were very expensive. This was a problem. Engineers needed to find a solution.

TONS OF TILES

Each space shuttle had more than 21,000 tiles. The tiles protected the shuttle from heat. Workers had to look at each one before every flight.

CHAPTER 3

THE
Falcon 9

The company SpaceX designs reusable rockets. Elon Musk started SpaceX in 2002. He is a businessman. He wants to make space travel cheaper. His goal was to make reusable rockets.

SpaceX rockets have launched from Texas, Florida, and California.

17

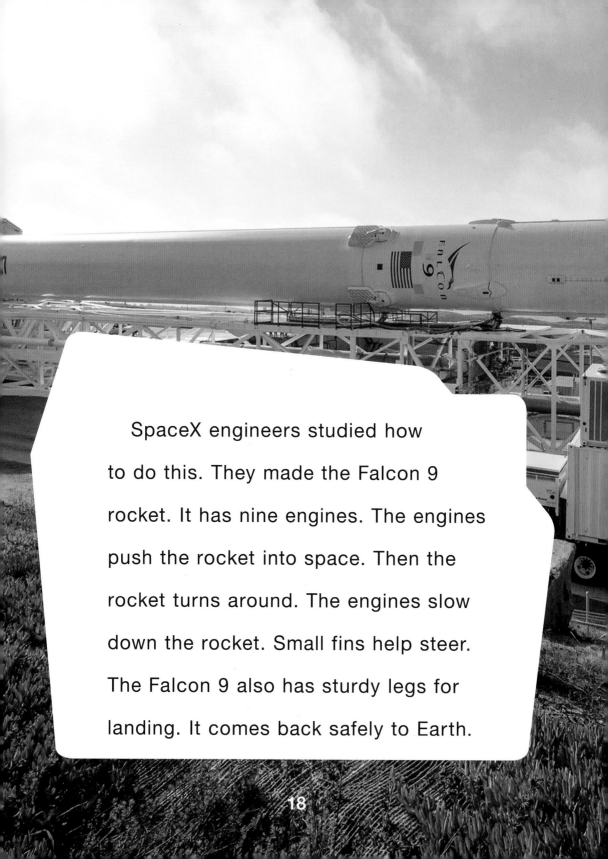

SpaceX engineers studied how to do this. They made the Falcon 9 rocket. It has nine engines. The engines push the rocket into space. Then the rocket turns around. The engines slow down the rocket. Small fins help steer. The Falcon 9 also has sturdy legs for landing. It comes back safely to Earth.

The Falcon 9
weighs more than
one million pounds
(450,000 kilograms).

SpaceX has also safely landed rockets on land.

STANDING STEADY

A rocket's engines can easily break. Sturdy metal legs support the rocket. The rocket stays steady. This keeps the engines safe. They can be used again.

SpaceX tested the Falcon 9 for years. Some rockets crashed. The company made history in 2015. A Falcon 9 launched from Florida. It delivered satellites into space. Then the rocket turned around. It fired its engines. Its fins steered. Flames shot from its center engine. The rocket slowed down. Its legs unfolded. It landed safely on the ground. Falcon 9 was the first rocket to do this.

CHAPTER 4

ROCKETS OF
the Future

Reusable rockets are the future. The Falcon 9 is just the beginning. Other companies are joining SpaceX. They are making their own reusable rockets.

SPACEX

SpaceX is working on new rockets.

They will be bigger than Falcon 9.

One will have 31 engines. It will carry

100 people into space.

Elon Musk wants to use his rockets to start a city on Mars.

ENCELA

BLUE ORIGIN

Jeff Bezos is another businessman. He is also interested in space. His rocket company is Blue Origin. It made the New Shepard rocket. New Shepard is smaller than the Falcon 9. It does not fly as high. It is not as fast. But it is much less expensive.

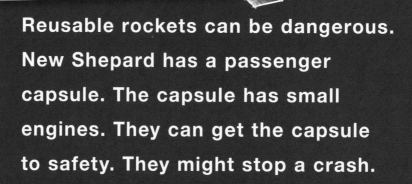

SAFETY FIRST

Reusable rockets can be dangerous. New Shepard has a passenger capsule. The capsule has small engines. They can get the capsule to safety. They might stop a crash.

Blue Origin wants
many people to
travel to space.

VIRGIN GALACTIC

Virgin Galactic is another rocket company. It made SpaceShipTwo. An aircraft carries SpaceShipTwo high in the air. Then SpaceShipTwo lights its rocket engine. It boosts into space. Passengers spend a few minutes there. Then the ship lands like an airplane.

SpaceShipTwo can carry passengers and two pilots.

Engineers are hard at work. They are improving rockets. New rockets will be cheaper. They will carry more people. They may even fly people to Mars!

GLOSSARY

engineer
a person who designs machines or structures

propellant
a material that rockets burn in their engines to push them forward

satellite
a human-made object that is launched into space and travels around Earth

Soviet Union
a former group of countries in Europe, including Russia and Ukraine

28

TRIVIA

1. The space shuttle *Discovery* flew more missions than any other shuttle. It went into space 39 times.

2. Elon Musk wants to use reusable rockets for more than space travel. He also wants to use them to fly between places on Earth. A rocket could carry people from New York to China in 40 minutes!

3. SpaceX launched 18 Falcon 9 rockets in 2017. It plans to launch even more each year in the future.

ACTIVITY

SpaceX puts videos of all its launches and landings on YouTube. Ask an adult to help you find one of these videos on the company's YouTube channel. Watch a mission from launch to landing. Then write your own description of everything the rocket does during this time. What things do you recognize from this book? What new things do you notice?

Next, think about how reusable rockets might affect you. Would you want to fly into space on a reusable rocket someday? Why or why not? Write about your opinion.

FURTHER RESOURCES

Want to learn more about the reusable rockets made by SpaceX and Blue Origin? Check out these websites:

Blue Origin's New Glenn Rocket
https://www.blueorigin.com/new-glenn

SpaceX's Failed Test
https://www.youtube.com/watch?v=bvim4rsNHkQ

SpaceX's Falcon 9 Rocket
http://www.spacex.com/falcon9

Interested in learning more about how rockets work? Take a look at these books:

Lock, Deborah. *Spaceships and Rockets*. New York: DK Publishing, 2016.

Morey, Allan. *Rockets*. Minneapolis, MN: Bellwether Media, 2018.

INDEX